Breathe Life Speak Life

(A Collection of Poems, Poetic Monologues & Spoken Word)

Margery Massena-Roach

Copyright

Breathe Life Speak Life

Copyright © 2015 by Margery Massena-Roach

Editing by Margery Massena-Roach.

All rights reserved in all media. No part of this book may be used or reproduced without written permission except in case of brief quotations embodied in critical articles and reviews.

Scripture quotations marked KJV are from the Holy Bible, King James Version (Authorized Version), first published in 1611. Quoted from the KJV Classic Reference Bible, Copyright © 1983 by The Zondervan Corporation.

The moral right of Margery Massena-Roach as the author of this work has been asserted by her in accordance with the Copyright, Designs, and Patents Act of 1988.

This is the work of Non-Fiction.
Cover Design: Joseph Roach
Published in the United States in 2015 by Margery Massena-Roach.

ISBN-13: 978-1516818259
ISBN-10: 1516818253

Acknowledgements

I must first give thanks to God, the head of my life. It is His spirit that speaks within me as I write. To my beautiful and selfless mother, Nicole Jerome, I love you so much mommy. Your endless love, sacrifice, and prayers have meant the world to me. I wish you could understand the depths of my love for you. To my affectionate husband, Joseph Roach, you are a powerhouse preacher and go-getter who never ceases to amaze me. I love you. Thank you for your unrelenting support, love, and friendship. We are two peas in a pod, and I am so happy to be your wife. To my friends, Colleen A. Roberts and Serrinea Granville, thank you for all of your advice. I appreciate and love you. To my in-laws, to all my dear friends, you are truly my angels. To Bishop, Micheal A. Mitchell, First Lady, Vivienne Mitchell, and New Life Tabernacle, thank you for your continuous encouragement and kindness. My heart is bursting with gratefulness. To the many people who've told me that I should write a book, thank you for believing in me. Last but not least, to the people who desire truth and enjoy the art of rhyming, this book is for you. There exists a real story behind every poem. My prayer is that you will be blessed.

Table of Contents

Acknowledgements iii
Table of Contents v
My Mother 1
A Great Man 2
The Child Inside (Spoken Word) 4
The Greatest Father 7
Graduation 9
For Pastors 10
The Cross Means More (Spoken Word) 11
Undefeated 15
A Union 17
Back to Eden 19
Darkness or Light 21
Greater Love 23
I am a Puppet 26
Our Sins 27
Refuse to Lose (Spoken Word) 28
Choose 30
Jesus, Christ 31

Grace	32
The Journey	33
Heartache	34
Answer the Call	35
Beware of the Thief	37
God's Gift	38
The Serpent (Poetic Monologue)	39
The Messiah (Poetic Monologue)	41
Ready or Not	43
Broken (Spoken Word)	46
Reflecting His Beauty	49
If Tombstones Could Talk	51
All or Nothing (Spoken Word)	53
The World's Jesus (Spoken Word)	58
About the Author	63

Who can find a virtuous woman? For her price is far above rubies.
(Proverbs 31:10, KJV)

My Mother

My mom always set a good example for me
We were always together; I was her sand, she was my sea
She dressed with finesse when she walked on the street
She would cover her body from her shoulders to her knees
Always classy and conservative, she'd say, "Only men wear pants."
After work, she involved me in all of her plans
She taught me right from wrong, and in anger, she didn't swear
We ended every night kneeling by the bedside in prayer
Every Sunday morning we would go to church together
Through the cold, scorching heat, snow, and even in rainy weather
My mom was strict, sometimes silly; she led a very simple life
She showed me how to cook and clean, she prepared me to be a wife
She worked hard in a foreign land where she got married and raised me
Her husband didn't stick around; I met him twice in New York City
She left school to be the best mother; she made time for childish games
She told me she loved me daily and gave me many nicknames
My mother is the illustration of the greatest courage and honor
She played two roles as both my mother and my father
I prayed that I would never marry someone like my dad
Who threw away the beautiful, virtuous woman that he had
On my wedding day, my mother gave me away
I'm grateful for a loving parent, a mom who taught me how to pray.

Blessed is the man that walketh not in the counsel of the ungodly, nor standeth in the way of sinners, nor sitteth in the seat of the scornful. But his delight is in the law of the Lord; and in his law doth he meditate day and night. And he shall be like a tree planted by the rivers of water, that bringeth forth his fruit in his season; his leaf also shall not wither; and whatsoever he doeth shall prosper. The ungodly are not so: but are like the chaff which the wind driveth away.
(Psalm 1:1-4, KJV)

A Great Man

A great man respects his mother, he has values and dignity
He does not make excuses and he works hard to succeed
With a head full of vision, he aspires to achieve
He respects women and he's there to raise his baby
A man won't join a gang since he knows what he's worth
If his family is in need, he will always put them first
He makes plans for the future, he doesn't live for just today
He's not afraid of commitment, he doesn't fit the cliché
Some boys won't go to school but sell drugs on a corner
A gun cocked, he got shot; now he's surrounded by mourners
He died in his youth because he chose to be violent
He's blessed with many gifts, but he never used his talents
He objectifies woman, moving from one girl to the next
Now he's worried about the results from his HIV test
He comes home most days around three in the morning
His parents lecture him but he never heeds their warning

Breathe Life Speak Life

He'd rather play a video game than get a book to read
He became a follower when he was meant to lead
He cuts school every week to hang out with his friends
His role models are deplorable; he looks up to the wrong men
He defines himself by his clothes and his sneakers
If he goes to church he never listens to the preacher
No example to guide him, his dad was never there to stand by him
Fathers, step up because your children need guiding!
He needs to see a reflection of what he should be
So he can be a great man and not a deadbeat
Single mothers are on their knees praying for their sons
Who won't stand for something and walk around with guns
Many boys waste away in inner cities everyday
Some would rather make easy money; "I'm a hustler" is what they say
Severe low self-esteem predispositions them to fail
And criminal activities have placed them in a jail
Birds of a feather look alike and flock together
Friends you keep can pull you down or make you better
I speak to the boys who cannot see their potential
You can climb a mountain, you can be influential!
God has given you the ability to succeed
To be the head and not the tail, to be above and not beneath
Boys, you can be anything you desire to be
You can overcome all obstacles, but first, you must believe.

Margery Massena-Roach

Come unto me, all ye that labor and are heavy laden,
and I will give you rest.
(Matthew 11:28, KJV)

The Child Inside (Spoken Word)

It happened in the summer on a hot sticky day
At the baby sitter's place
He was an old stout man; I can still see his face
He put his lips on my mouth and he said, "Give me a taste."
He had found me standing there, a small and innocent victim
Time ceased to exist as this tall man entered the kitchen
And his eyes looked so wild, with evil they glistened
He was drunk, his eyes were red, and his clothes were sloppy
It felt like time was in slow motion as he grabbed my body
And he looked at me like it was his favorite hobby
Then he pressed his mouth roughly against mine
My heart beat really hard in my chest, I was nine
It rapidly palpitated, seemingly two seconds away from flat lining
With fear.
I was in sheer
Terror, I could smell the strong scent of beer
On his breath, for some reason
I couldn't even
Manage to scream for help
It was as if I was gagged
By this living, breathing, moving red flag,

Breathe Life Speak Life

Melting on my skin
A bass drum in
My chest was pounding
Every noise in my surroundings
Sounding
Like echoes under water and
I was trapped in the hand
Of the Bogeyman
I was frozen like a deer with headlights in its eyes
And wished someone would rescue me from this plight.
In shock and feeling so sick
To the pit
Of my nine-year-old stomach,
I felt his tongue thrust
As his hands touched
Me, my fingers clutched air
And feet became anchors, every hair
Stood on end
Then
Somehow, all of a sudden
I could move
I pushed through
His clutch, running into the bathroom,
Falling with disbelief
To my knees
Scrubbing everywhere he touched till it bleeds
I needed so desperately
To get this disgusting, horrible, and shameful feeling
Off of me.

Margery Massena-Roach

How many people have a story that is worse than this?
So they try to control things because back then they were helpless
Now his behavior is reckless
And his past has the answer
He is like this because these memories are a cancer
A mass of death
Growing inside till it stifles his breath
He thought he buried the past but it grins on the back shelf
Of his mind, within he'll find his nine-year-old self
He is trapped at the age of that child who was so afraid
That child who has now become an adult filled with rage
But if he would only reach deep within
And allow a person who cares to listen
He could break down the bars of this emotional prison
Exposing the wound will help him to heal
He bottles up his pain so he's unable to feel
He has been doing everything he could do to try to numb it
He can run for so long but he can't really hide from it
He can lay it down at the altar
Give it all to his Heavenly Father
God can mend every wound, to the hurting He's a doctor
His past can be behind him and God can help him to receive
The healing and freedom that the nine-year-old child within him really
Needs.

And [I] will be a Father unto you, and ye shall be my sons
and daughters, saith the Lord Almighty.
(2 Corinthians 6:18, KJV)

The Greatest Father

Our Father which art in Heaven, you are the example of a "dad"
You gave all your children the most prized possession that you had
Jehovah Jirah, you're our provider because you gave to us in need
You sacrificed yourself so that we wouldn't have to bleed
You gave us words of wisdom so we'd walk the right way
You never abandoned us because you promised that you would stay
You protected us from harm; you shielded us from danger
You welcomed a relationship so we wouldn't know you as a stranger
You kept the family together; you were there in dreary weather
You extended grace and mercy in times we should have known better
You hurt with us in our pain, provided shelter from the storm and rain
You looked beyond our mistakes, and you erased the shame
Your love is unconditional and we appreciate all you've done
We can tell you anything, you see where we're coming from
You have listened to our cries and bring comfort, you really care
You welcome us with open arms and you are always there
You've never left our side and you are always involved
We look to you for solutions to problems we need to solve
Your faithfulness remains, your compassion stays the same
Yesterday, today, and forevermore you never change
God, you showed us how every earthly father is supposed to be

Margery Massena-Roach

You gave them the perfect guide on how to love and how to lead
You are our closest friend, our comforter, and dad
Thank you for being the greatest father we've ever had!

The soul of the sluggard desireth, and hath nothing: but the soul of the diligent shall be made fat.
(Proverbs 13:4, KJV)

Graduation

Behind a classroom desk, taking multiple choice tests
Wordy essays and pop quizzes
Studying demanding subjects like Calculus, Statistics
Chemistry, Biology and Physics
Reviewing for a midterm as you also learn French or Spanish
Taking notes, English class quotes, and a very effective study habit
They all lead to the day that you can say, "I have finally made it!"
After the trials you've experienced, you have now graduated.
All of your hard work has paid off just like you anticipated
Congratulations on your graduation! This is a cause for a celebration
You now have a powerful weapon in your hand called an education
Although it seemed so far away, you now wear your gown and cap
As you walk down the aisle to take your seat, you hear friends and families clap
After working diligently, it feels great to finally achieve
You are blessed, you're a success, and you kept at it because you believed
You survived so many challenges and your future is now shining bright
Today is only just the beginning of the rest or your life
The education you have received can open many doors
Continue to dream; be what you want to be, the opportunity is all Yours.

Margery Massena-Roach

And we beseech you, brethren, to know them which labor among you, and are over you in the Lord, and admonish you; And to esteem them very highly in love for their work's sake...
(1 Thessalonians 5:12, 13, KJV)

For Pastors

A special thanks to our pastor who oversees the church and serves
He is a shepherd to the flock, he shares the daily Word
He leads with spiritual wisdom, he prays with sincere concern
He preaches truth and from all sin, he urges us to turn
He's caring, extending mercy and helping those who are in need
His main goal is to guide us to long life eternally
He tells us to be holy and to turn away from wrong
He provides encouragement so that we may be strong
He strives for excellence, he leads with all humility
He's a light in this dark world, an example for all to see
He's faithful; he is passionate, always giving his very best
His preaching brings conviction, to come to God in brokenness
He makes us smile often and gives a word that stirs emotion
The sermons that he delivers are always thought provoking
He doesn't give up on us; he holds our hands when we are down
His anointing breaks chains, setting free all those who are bound
His roles are countless; he's a husband, a father, and friend to many
If we searched the world to find a better pastor we never would find any!

Howbeit in vain do they worship me, teaching for doctrines the commandments of men. For laying aside the commandment of God, ye hold the tradition of men, as the washing of pots and cups: and many other such like things ye do. And he said unto them, Full well ye reject the commandment of God, that ye may keep your own tradition.
(Mark 7: 7-9, KJV)

The Cross Means More (Spoken Word)

We've come dressed to impress
Like on a holiday
When store displays
Are all engraved
With furry bunnies and colored eggs
Laid inside of a nest
The church will be full of guests
They'll have on their Sunday's best
Some say it's the way to celebrate the cross.

People will take a short drive to arrive
With a few to the pews
Where the preacher will teach us
About the Savior called Jesus
Some say it's the way to celebrate the cross.

Many families gather together every Sunday or once a year,
And they sit together so they could hear

Margery Massena-Roach

God's Word,
Something they heard
In the past before
Its impact faded fast after walking out the door
Many went to church to give reverence to the Lord
There are those who came to reflect
While others came to pay God due respect
Some say it's the way to celebrate the cross.

At the altar, we pray that God forgives us, a sinner
After the sermon we head off to eat Sunday dinner
Then we go on our way
Until the next event or holiday
Some say it's the way to celebrate the cross.

To some the cross is a fashion statement to wear upon their chests
But God doesn't desire emblems; He said our obedience is best
And that it's in righteousness and fellowship with Him that we truly
Honor our Savior's death
For the resurrection and the cross has more value than a chain
Because it's a reminder that Jesus can save
The cross reminds us of God's love that gave,
That He rose from the grave,
And He came to give us a second chance
It was a saving plan
Made for all of humanity.

The cross is celebrated each day we're alive,
Each day the flesh dies
And scales fall from the eyes,

Breathe Life Speak Life

Each day that someone cries
Out to the master,
And leaves the pleasures of sin to go after
God and His righteousness
Yes,
His death and resurrection means more than a day!
It means more than what we say
And more than that one moment we prayed,
More than us saying that we want to change
But never exchange
The old garments for the new and still remain the same.

The cross is really celebrated
When Christ is elevated
And His sacrifice is really commemorated
And our love is really demonstrated
When we surrender to the King
Who came just to bring
Salvation that washes away all sin!

Let the cross mean more
To you than before
Know it's the cross that gives us power to fight in this spiritual war
Let His Holy Spirit pour
Out and fill you,
Until you
Know Him as more than just a higher power who sits above
God doesn't just love you, *God is love*
Let His sacrifice on the cross mean that you leave the world behind
In order to find

The resurrection and the life
Who is Jesus Christ.

For this life is like
A flower that fades
Tomorrow is not promised but you have today
Today is the day you can receive the grace
Within the arms of the Savior
So let the cross mean more,
Much more than before
Let it mean you have a relationship with Christ and that your salvation
Is really sure
He said if you suffer for His sake, you shall reign with Him forever
More
And if you endure temptation the crown of life will then be yours
Knowing this would be the best way to celebrate the cross.

And he said unto me, My grace is sufficient for thee: for my strength is made perfect in weakness. Most gladly therefore will I rather glory in my infirmities, that the power of Christ may rest upon me.
(2 Corinthians 12:19, KJV)

Undefeated

This year for many was a challenge
Through bruises and blows here we stand undefeated
Triumphant, at times depleted
Afflicted and often mistreated
Yet here we are, still strong and undefeated
Despite it all, God has blessed us
And through hardships He has kept us
He lifted us up when we were faint, never retreating
The righteous were not forsaken
The walls around us were shaking
The pressure was great
But we kept the faith
Still undefeated
He gave strength to the weak
He was right there when we needed
Him, we can declare that we have not been defeated
His angels held us up when we dashed against a stone
He stepped down to earth from His throne
To give victory to the defeated
God took on human form

Margery Massena-Roach

From a virgin He was born
As He died the temple curtain was torn
In two, He died for all of the defeated
He perished on a hill
And on a wooden cross He was killed
He rose and sent His Holy Spirit to fill
Us, so we'd remain undefeated
He is the living water that quenches our thirst
Seek ye first His kingdom, in Christ we are completed
At the right hand He is seated,
Full of strength and power, every knee
Shall bow to Christ who is undefeated
One God, one name
Now and forever He is the same,
Jesus is full of humility while Satan is conceited
Our eyes up like amid Christ's ascension
Enter into a third dimension
Every champion will one day meet Him
And with open arms they'll all be greeted.

But now are they many members, yet but one body. And the eye cannot say unto the hand, I have no need of thee: nor again the head to the feet, I have no need of you. Nay, much more those members of the body, which seem to be more feeble, are necessary:
(1 Corinthians 12:20-22, KJV)

A Union

How good and how pleasant it is for brethren to dwell in unity,
To esteem each other better than themselves, to become a community
When saints meet, they can connect, working together as a team
We must unite, with faith we'll strive, this is the Year of Jubilee
We've joined, merging together as we move with strength and power
Christ gives us confidence we need to build within this hour
Because this is the moment for the church to come alive
I pray for you, and you pray for me, I need you to survive
Let's support each other as we work to grow God's kingdom
By reading His Word, with consistent prayer, we will increase in wisdom
Let's put aside our differences and let us learn to love each other
In Christ we've become a family; we're sisters and we're brothers
I say *I am* my brother's keeper, Cain may not agree
I care about what you go through; you mean that much to me
Let's hold hands as we make plans because divided we will fall
Together we can stand as we pursue the higher call
In one place with one accord is where great things can happen
The power of the Holy Ghost will work as we take action
Amos chapter three verse three, *how can two walk lest they agree?*

Margery Massena-Roach

As saints, we march together, as believers, we yoke equally
Let's have a revival and let us let go of every idol
Let us put away the strife and let us take up The Holy Bible
Let's put an end to bickering, the gossip and division
Let's portray the Christ within us through the life that we are living
Christ is the head; we are the body, so the spirit makes us one
We are a force to reckon with if we become a union.

For as in Adam all die, even so in Christ shall all be made alive.
(1 Corinthians 15:22, KJV)

Back to Eden

Suppose Adam and Eve refused to eat from the forbidden tree?
What if Eve never believed the tricks Satan had up his sleeve?
What if she quickly took off when
The Serpent lied and she never sinned?
But obeyed God and lived in innocence
Because she saw Satan's pretense?
If we could rewind time back to that day
And Adam and Eve had never strayed,
Sewed fig leaves because of shame,
Then we would be in the perfect place
Let's go back to Eden
Before any men became heathen
Before our own lust weakened us, and Jesus had to free men
We would be in the garden in perfect harmony and peace
There would be no chains of bondage, we would all be free
There would be no disease like cancer and aids
We would never ever worry because we'd never be afraid
There would be no hospitals because we'd never get sick
There'd be no Holocaust or humans hoarded on slave ships
There would be no hunger, poverty, and stress
We would never have funerals because there would be no death
There'd be no hate, no hurt, and no pain,

Margery Massena-Roach

No emotions like anxiety, guilt, embarrassment or shame
There'd be no segregation, no Ku Klux Klan,
No world war one and two, no terrorist plans,
Natural disasters like tornadoes and earthquakes,
No separation of church and state, we'd all have one faith,
No human trafficking or rape, no envy or vanity,
Jealousy, pride, or violence in humanity,
No Kleenex napkins because we would never cry,
No mafias or genocide, no gangs or suicide,
No famine and affliction, people without houses,
Children having children, domestically abusive spouses,
Sexual perversion, drunkenness, and addiction
Christ wouldn't have died because there'd be no crucifixion
If we could only reverse what happened back then
Before Adam and Eve committed humanity's first sin
That day in the Garden of Eden.

For such are false apostles, deceitful workers, transforming themselves into the apostles of Christ. And no marvel; for Satan himself is transformed into an angel of light.
(2 Corinthians 11: 13, 14, KJV)

Darkness or Light

The darkness is like an invisible cloud
It shuts down your consciousness as it surrounds
When you are exposed, you may not even know
But sooner or later the side effects show
It gives the illusion that it's no big deal
But the truth of the matter is that lies are concealed
What you think is harmless is what may have bound you
Open your eyes to what's really around you
It's not a natural but a spiritual war
And it's something that people shouldn't ignore
Who has authority over your mind?
Are you exposed to darkness or light?

The darkness can glow; it's a show to deceive
Cunning and crafty, the serpent tricks you like Eve
The glitz and the glamour and the call from within
It's the attempt from the devil to get you to sin
He'll come as beautiful angel of light
And make you believe that the darkness is right
He'll mess with your mind till you fall for the game

Margery Massena-Roach

The darkness eventually will bring you pain
Then slowly you'll drown, an abyss with no end
Because you gave darkness the room to come in
Who has authority over your mind?
Are you exposed to darkness or light?

If you're in darkness, you're far from the light
God does not judge by what we think is right
Whatever you lift above Christ is your God
Its innocent face is the devil's facade
The world glorifies people and things
But all of the glory belongs to the King!
We're in the world but He says where not of it
Here there's lust of the flesh and people who covet
No matter what you've done, you may be afar
God wants your companionship; you are His heart
Who has authority over your mind?
Are you exposed to darkness or light?

If you follow the light, you will surely be blessed
He'll help you through trials, temptations, and tests
Jesus is the light leading to life everlasting
Everything here on earth will all soon be passing
He wants a relationship and not mere acquaintance
He hung on the cross; His love is so blatant
His spirit must fill you, for His purpose He'll use you
Read His Word so that the darkness cannot confuse you
Who has authority over your mind?
Are you exposed to darkness or light?

For I am persuaded, that neither death, nor life, nor angels, nor principalities, nor powers, nor things present, nor things to come, nor height, nor depth, nor any other creature, shall be able to separate us from the love of God, which is in Christ Jesus our Lord.
(Romans 8:38, 39, KJV)

Greater Love

I am so in love with you, you're omniscient, majesty
I admire you and desire to make you extremely happy
You have set me free and your love for me is exhilarating
I've received your perfect peace, it's so invigorating
I am infatuated because you are so amazing
I have learned that people change but you are never changing
I give my life, a sacrifice to give true worship to your name
My heart is beating for the King, and I have never been the same
Since you came in I've found true love, it's all I need and so much more
I never, ever felt a precious and pure love like this before!
I want to shout on roof tops nonstop, let the world know how I feel
When I received your Holy Spirit, I knew for sure that you are real
Immersed in your love, it makes me want to live this Christian life
You are like a husband to me; I am your submissive wife
Like romantic clichés, your love for me I would say is…
A long walk on the beach, it's like Song of Solomon poetry
Like a dozen roses given to me or diamonds, bright and shining
Your love's a walk in the park when flowers bloom in springtime
Or a view of the skyline, like a rainbow in sunshine

Margery Massena-Roach

It's like watching the sunset on a date with a mate
Or the rush of emotion when two lovers embrace
Jesus, you proposed to me with mercy and with grace
With your life, long life, and mansions in a heavenly place
You're like Jacob who worked fourteen years first, so he could marry Rachel
Like a knight in shining armor you came riding, strong and faithful
You wooed me with your love story like a dinner by candlelight
Like an old couple, married for years, some say we look alike
I long to know you intimately in holy matrimony so divine
See, love for you is not just another word, rehearsed like a pick-up line
"I love you" seems to be three words that have lost its meaning
Father, help us understand that love is more than just a feeling.

I apologize for times I've pleased myself and let you down
My heart was torn after I turned to foolishness I'd found
I'll serve you Lord, Jesus Christ until my body joins the earth
You came in and changed my life, so I will always put you first
You are why I can go on, and you're the reason why I sing
The fame and fortune of this world don't measure up to all you bring
For you loved the world so much you gave your one, only begotten Son
Despite of how we treated you and sinful things that we have done
Like a friend with great love, you gave your life for friends
While we were yet like enemies, came short, immoral men
On the cross you said, "Forgive them for they know not what they do."
In so much pain, flesh torn and blood-stained, you loved me before I Knew you
You left your throne, came to your own, but they did not receive you
You paid our debt when you freely let creation pierce and beat you
You say love thy neighbor as thyself, this is your command

Forgive them for the things they've done as God's forgiven man
Abba, I ask you to help me to bless those who have cursed me,
To do good to those who've hurt me and to enemies who've coerced
Me
To pray for men who have accused me, persecute, or use me
To show the perfect love of God if people have abused me
Lord, you said if I despise my brother who is next to me,
How can I love God who is a spirit that I cannot see?
Though I speak with tongues of men and of angels and have not charity
I am a sounding brass, cymbals tinkering very loudly
"I love you" seems to be three words that have lost its meaning
Father, help us understand that love is more than just a feeling!

But in a great house there are not only vessels of gold and of silver, but also of wood and of earth; and some to honor, and some to dishonor. If a man therefore purge himself from these, he shall be a vessel unto honor, sanctified, and meet for the master's use, and prepared unto every good work.
(2 Timothy 2:20-21, KJV)

I am a Puppet

I want to be a puppet in your hands, Father, to use
Animate, operate and move me as you choose
Take control; I'll do your will, going to where you lead me
Your Word, a lamp to light my path; the tempter won't deceive me
Without you I'm incapable, it's your Holy Ghost and fire
That moves upon me, speaks within to guide me and inspire
Anoint me for your purpose; fill my cup to the brim
From this world, I'll stand out, never to blend in
Let my own desires crumble, so I can die to the flesh
Receive all the glory, let your power manifest
Never will I be a tool for Satan's use
I will use all gifts given to bring glory to you
I give you praise, I worship you in spirit and in truth
With all the strength you've given, when I'm old and in my youth.
I want a life that's set apart, committed to the Lord
Take out what's not perfect and throw pride overboard
If I make my kingdom come, it will surely fall
Attached to strings pulled by the King, I am a puppet doll.

For all have sinned, and come short of the glory of God.
(Romans 3:23, KJV)

Our Sins

Our sins are like the chains they wrapped around Jesus as they dragged
Him to meet a punishment He didn't deserve
Our sins caused the shame that He felt as He was condemned to death
And creation observed
Our sins are like the hands that tore His beard from His face, our sins
Are like the spit that flew from their lips
Our sins are like the soldiers that gambled His clothes away, our sins
Are like the betrayal of Judas' kiss
Our sins are like the cross He carried up the hill, and the nails entering
Each foot and each hand
Our sins caused Jesus' blood to be spilled, our God was despised and
Rejected by man
Our sins are like the fists that struck Him; our sins are like the crown of
Thorns instead of gold
Our sins caused the pain that racked His body, and His loved ones
Wept in anguish, unable to be consoled.
Our sins caused Him to be buried in a tomb, in the heart of the earth,
He rose after three days
There was a great cost to our sins, but when the accuser came to indict
Us, Jesus Christ could say, "The debt has been paid."

Margery Massena-Roach

I can do all things through Christ which strengtheneth me.
(Philippians 4:13, KJV)

Refuse to Lose (Spoken Word)

What does tomorrow hold?
How will my future unfold?
I wonder what God has in store for me
What has He called me to do?
What does He want me to be?
The earth is the Lord's, He gives us the best
He wants us to prosper and have good success
Seeking first the kingdom
I will ask God for wisdom
I refuse to lose.

It seems that unhappy people always choose to settle.
Many are content with having the bronze instead of the gold medal.
Why not push for more
And press beyond the closed door?
Overcome all oppression.
Take steps towards progression.
We must first believe
Ask, seek, and knock, then you will receive
Many goals we hope to reach
But what is lacking
Is a jolt of passion
And our action

Breathe Life Speak Life

Behind the words.

Faith without works is dead
And execution is more important than words that are said
Our dreams
Are like steam
That escapes in the breeze
If we do nothing to build it
It's as if we have killed it
Our dream is like a person
To survive it needs nourishment
Without a vision, people perish.
Every vision should be cherished.
To God, earthly dreams are important
Although you must have dreams with spiritual merit.

As I swim against the stream
I ask God to breathe on me
Grant me favor
As I labor
And guide every decision
Because favor is greater than any blessings given
I refuse to lose.

Even though I can't see it clearly
I'll hold on to the dream dearly
I'll speak life to every vision
It's the reason why I am living
I exist not just to be
But to breathe life to dreams.

Margery Massena-Roach

And Elijah came unto all the people, and said, How long halt ye between two opinions? If the LORD be God, follow him: but if Baal, then follow him. And the people answered him not a word.
(1 Kings 18:21, KJV)

Choose

Two choices ahead, a decision needs to be made
It's either you take the narrow path or you choose the broad way
Because if you have two masters, then to sin you are a slave
It will rule your life and only lead you to the grave
The weakness of the flesh and illusions of grandeur
Are tools Satan uses, he will lie in every answer
You are his prey, and he will creep up like a panther
He is sly, subtle, and subliminal in his manner
Purgatory is fiction, there's Heaven and the lake of fire
The latter was for demons and for the devil who is a liar
But we disobeyed; in rebellion we sought our own desires
God came to set us free when we got tangled in the brier
We choose our destination based on who we choose to follow
There's a consequence to choice; that's a tough pill for some to swallow
You should choose God today because it might be too late tomorrow.

For God so loved the world, that he gave his only begotten Son, that whosoever believeth in him should not perish, but have everlasting life.
(John 3:16, KJV)

Jesus, Christ

We were born into sin and for sure we'd be lost
If the Lord did not come, pay the price on the cross
Our God had a plan with a purpose to die
So the world could have access to eternal life
God put on a body and lived among His people
He cast out demons and healed those who were feeble
He cleansed the lepers, rose men from the dead
He cured paralytics and fed five thousand men
He walked on water and He turned water to wine
He opened deaf ears and the eyes of the blind
His disciple betrayed Him and soldiers bound Him
A crowd charged Him guilty although He was innocent
They made Him carry a cross, on His head, they placed thorns,
Gave Him gall to drink, beat Him until He was deformed
They spit in His face, they mocked Him and jeered,
His hands, His feet, and His side were pierced
His blood covered our sins; He was bruised for all our iniquities,
Chastised for our peace, by His stripes we are healed
Jesus rose on the third day; evil's minion couldn't win
O grave, where is your victory? O death, where is your sting?

Margery Massena-Roach

Come now, and let us reason together, saith the LORD: though your sins be as scarlet, they shall be as white as snow; though they be red like crimson, they shall be as wool.
(Isaiah 1:18, KJV)

Grace

She walks with a flair and sticks her chest out in the air
Her clothes must always show her curves, hips, and derriere
All the passersby stare, men whistle at her on the streets
She paints an image to hide the deep void and insecurities
Her soul screams for attention, false confidence is on her face
She only lives for the next high and she looks forward to the chase
She is trapped in a nightmare, running, and never feeling secure
She chooses the wrong men because the wrong men chose her
She trades her body for love she wants but she won't ever earn
Men used her and left her broken, never giving real love in return
If she could only see that she could change her destiny
She could be a real trophy who is covered in God's glory
Christ is who she really needs, He loves her, and He'll console her.
If only she would just reach out, and not let her past control her.
Like Mary, she could weep, and pour perfume on Christ's feet
She would know she can be forgiven and go on her way merrily.
God can satisfy her, not the things that she was chasing after
Love the world had given her, she would realize was made of plaster
Her life will only change when she finally seeks God's face
She is not her mistakes; she will be a trophy of grace.

Though I walk through the valley of the shadow of death, I will fear no evil: for thou art with me; thy rod and thy staff they comfort me.
(Psalm 23:4, KJV)

The Journey

This journey is rough, but He said, "I am able.
Know I am here when your path is unstable
Sorrows will only endure for a night
The morning brings joy, my comfort and light.
The journey was also not easy for me
My hands that uphold you were nailed to a tree
But I am your strength and I'll be your guide
When you feel all alone, I am right by your side
Your faith will be tested, but don't give up ever
At the end of this journey you will live forever."

Margery Massena-Roach

And God shall wipe away all tears from their eyes; and there shall be no more death, neither sorrow, nor crying, neither shall there be any more pain: for the former things are passed away.
(Revelation 21:4, KJV)

Heartache

When we think of the disaster, the only thing we feel is pain
There's no sunshine, we're drenched now; we were left out in the rain
We have mourned; we have wept because of the loss that was endured
But we have kept the faith; we know in God we are secure
Though troubled on every side, we are not distressed
Not walking in despair though our minds may be perplexed
Persecuted, not forsaken, cast down but not destroyed
Hearts are broken, but still remaining faithful to the Lord
God has the answers to every troubling circumstance
Although the reason may be difficult to see and understand
We have faced destruction, we have experienced devastation
But it's only temporary; we have a great mansion waiting
In Heaven, God's prepared a place, one day for us to see
No more pain and suffering, no more anguish or misery
That day the Lord will wipe away the tears from every eye
Death and sorrow will cease, we will kiss this world goodbye
We must run with patience this race that is set before us
God has kept His promises, His true Word reassures us
Although we've suffered greatly, for our peace, God paid the cost
In Christ, things work together in our heartache and in loss.

Therefore said he unto them, the harvest truly is great, but the laborers are few: pray ye therefore the Lord of the harvest, that he would send forth laborers into his harvest.
(Luke 10:2, KJV)

Answer the Call

The spirit grieves
As I keep ignoring this call;
I have shut my ears spiritually
I am the sheep
That went halfway
To the Shepard's dismay
I delayed when I heard His voice leading me
My heart is swaddled in fear
Yet His still small voice speaks and I can softly hear
Him urging me to go
My soul says yes
While my flesh
Is telling Him no
For too long, I have been hesitant;
It's shut up like Jeremiah,
Quickening fire
Like an accelerant
I never meant to disobey
But this call caused me to be afraid
And like Jonah, I ran from the call in an attempt to get away

Until I realized that this call is not about me
Because this call was intended to set someone free.
This call is for that woman who thought about suicide
This call is for that single parent who sheds tears at night
This call is for that young man who has become an addict
This call is for that girl whose life has been so tragic
For that teen with low self-esteem
For the spiritually hungry
This call goes beyond my capacity to see
I will answer this call; this call will impact destinies.

The thief cometh not, but for to steal, and to kill, and to destroy: I am come that they might have life, and that they might have it more abundantly.
(John 10:10, KJV)

Beware of the Thief

Every saint of the Most High, you must beware
We're in combat with the prince of the power of the air
Put the whole armor on, have the sword of the spirit drawn
The King is coming, and He will expose Satan as a con
Don't be fooled by the disguise or the candy-coated lies
The itching ears of people listen, without questioning would buy
The world's beauty has wooed some; blemishes are hid with make-up
As the bridegroom tarries, let us oil our lamps and wake up
God's people are perishing because of knowledge that they lack
They're oblivious to the war because they're blind to the attack
We must pray in the spirit that God removes the many blindfolds
And that the weapons of our warfare will pull down every stronghold.

Margery Massena-Roach

For by grace are ye saved through faith; and that not of yourselves: it is the gift of God: Not of works, lest any man should boast.
(Ephesians 2:8-9, KJV)

God's Gift

By faith we are saved,
Through God's gift of grace
Because of mercy He gave,
Our sins can be erased
God bore the shame and He was disgraced
Death was sin's payment but He took our place
He was nailed upon a tree
After being beaten brutally
Peter denied Him three times
He was accused of lies
Judas Iscariot betrayed Him
He could've called angels to save Him
But He showed love to those who blamed Him.
They heard Him saying, *"Forgive them Father…"*
He was given vinegar instead of water
It was just like a lamb that the Son was led to the slaughter.

Be sober, be vigilant; because your adversary the devil, as a roaring lion, walketh about, seeking whom he may devour.
(1 Peter 5:8, KJV)

The Serpent (Poetic Monologue)

"You idiotic fools and you powerless buffoons
You're gullibility is amazing, watch me skillfully defeat you!
O, what distaste! You don't deserve mercy and grace
I want to destroy you and devour up your useless brainless face!
My plans are to dethrone the Great One who is mighty
With evil I will replace righteousness and piety
Every knee should bow to me, just look at all I've done!
I have wreaked much havoc, I should be number one!
I could never figure out why God loves you foolish creatures
I work to crush your faith; I have soldiers and false teachers
I have some power, I am strong. I want to take those Christians down
I want to tear them up to pieces; track them like a bloodhound!
I will do all I'm allowed so they can lose their stubborn faith
I want to send strong winds and fire to see them finally shake!
My spirits in high places have worked to cause confusion
Ha-ha! (Laughing evilly 4 times) This war is raging, and I'm not losing!
I will mess with their minds; I want to crush them with my teeth
I want to beat them into batter; I want to sift them like wheat!
I will make them think the lake of fire is one big party
So I can sneak up like a lion and crush their puny bodies!
I'll persist with wicked trysts, those weak beings can't resist!

Margery Massena-Roach

The sin is in their nature and darkness is their bliss
If I could twist their fragile spines until I hear a snap
I know that they would curse God and quickly turn their backs!
I despise all God's disciples who try to cast me out
When I leave this vessel, I'll try to come back with a crowd!
I love to take what's true and add a little lie (chuckling evilly)
People fall for my gimmicks and they easily comply!
I scratch their every itch; most are turned off by the truth
That is why thousands of people are very easily fooled!
I'm coming to attack; all of my demons have my back
I will use problems, music, temptation, and lust as my trap
The Antichrist is coming soon to reign, to have some power
I am working every second, every minute, and every hour
I see how pleasure is what most of these humans have pursued
I will use it to pound to pulp all of these pathetic fools!"

For the Son of man is come to seek and to save that which was lost.
(Luke 19:10, KJV)

The Messiah (Poetic Monologue)

"Come unto me, ye heavy laden; ye that labor
For I will give you rest, I am God, I am your Savior
I have proved my love for you, for sin, I was the sacrifice
I am the way, I am the truth, and I, Jesus, am the life
Your soul won't be satisfied by the pleasures here on earth
I am the living water, drink of me, and you won't thirst
Great plans I have for you, thoughts of good and not of evil
Look unto me for help; I provide strength to all my people
The problems that you face can't compare to joy you'll have
Great things I have prepared; your future's better than your past
Many souls are on the line, they haven't yet made up their minds
I need you to make a difference; they are running out of time
The harvest is plenteous, but the laborers are few
So make haste my child, it is important that I use you!
My spirit will work within you, turning people from their sins
They all have a greater purpose, every single one of them!
The enemy has tried his very best to use deception
He is lying every day to keep souls out of Heaven
There are lessons you must learn, you will suffer for my sake
But all things will work together to keep you from the fiery lake
Satan tries to blind the minds of men so they can't see my light

Margery Massena-Roach

Have your loins girt about with truth and let it shine bright
Remain faithful, trust in me, and be instant in every season
Let the world know of my love, that I give life, and I bring healing."

Knowing this first, that there shall come in the last days scoffers, walking after their own lusts, and saying, where is the promise of his coming? For since the fathers fell asleep, all things continue as they were from the beginning of the creation. For this they willingly are ignorant of, that by the word of God the heavens were of old, and the earth standing out of the water and in the water: Whereby the world that then was, being overflowed with water, perished: But the heavens and the earth, which are now, by the same word are kept in store, reserved unto fire against the day of judgment and perdition of ungodly men. But, beloved, be not ignorant of this one thing, that one day is with the Lord as a thousand years, and a thousand years as one day. The Lord is not slack concerning his promise, as some men count slackness; but is longsuffering to us-ward, not willing that any should perish, but that all should come to repentance. But the day of the Lord will come as a thief in the night; in which the heavens shall pass away with a great noise, and the elements shall melt with fervent heat, the earth also and the works that are therein shall be burned up.
(2 Peter 3:3-10 KJV)

Ready or Not

The ground shakes and the earth quakes; it breaks for the sake of Christ's coming
False teachers arise with many lies and saints have been succumbing
Phony prophets will fill their pockets by seducing those who are saved
Great signs from Heaven, Matthew twenty-four verse eleven did
Forewarn us of these wicked days

Jesus said there'd be wars and rumors of wars, and nations fighting
Against nations
Iniquity will abound, so the love of many will wax cold among all
Creation
Children will rise against parents; there'll be famines, and pestilence,
Fearful sights, people saying they're Christ, and so much death and
Violence
As prophesied, the beginnings of sorrows are happening this very
Moment
We must always be ready and we must not be spiritually dormant
Jesus Christ is coming soon; many may say He is way overdue
Just know a thousand years might be long to us but to God it's only a
Few
God has His own time system, so don't fall victim to the enemy's lies
God waits for many men to repent; this is why He has not yet arrived
Yet He said He'd shorten the days because if not, the elect will begin to
Stray
In the twinkling of an eye, at the trumpet's cry every man will see His
Face
How many times do we hear God's voice and make the choice to turn
Him away?
We say that we're not quite ready for a change and that we'll come back
Another day
But whether we are ready or not, the creator of the universe will still
Return
With the cares of life and distractions everywhere, many are not even
Concerned
That day He will not take any excuses if we refused Him to choose our
Own way

So we must be ready every moment, we must be prepared every day
No one knows the hour of His coming; it will be like a thief in the night
So let us long for His salvation; let His law be our delight.

Margery Massena-Roach

He healeth the broken in heart, and bindeth up their wounds.
(Psalm 147:3, KJV)

Broken (Spoken Word)

I've been broken and shattered into bits and pieces
I can't really believe this
It's hard for me to breathe, this
Pain is suffocating me
Like a pillow held and violently
Pressed to my face
Now I'm left in a dark place
And in torment, it's the worst case
My life has ever seen,
To be so broken that I bleed
I have been cut so brutally
As if my jugular vein has been split
My lungs constrict
And heart is ripped
And torn
The world regrets the day that this child was ever born
I am emotionally deformed
I now sit here all alone
In this pain.

Save me from myself.
This hurt is like a poison I am drinking to my death

Breathe Life Speak Life

As I hide behind the facade of this mask that I have kept
These nights I have barely slept
Because this heart is weeping
Inside this heart is leaking
Shredded and battered, all tattered, and profusely bleeding
My grief's on rewind from these thoughts that keep repeating
I'm wishing today that this heart just stops beating
As I stand here all alone in this pain.

Why did this happen? How did I find myself here?
I have searched all over but there is nobody there
I'm on the edge of giving up, it feels like nobody cares
I am surrounded by disaster
I wish I could be numb, I wish these wounds would heal faster
I am shackled like a slave and this pain has been my master
Every root of bitterness
To my bones is brittleness
That have transformed into wickedness
To help me feel this pain less.

This plagues me like a ghost haunting present and past
I am like a fractured bone, in fragments with no cast
I heard someone say that this pain too shall pass
Yet I long for death to take me
But He says this pain will make me
This pain was not to break me
He said He won't forsake me
And that He
Wraps His arms around me
In this pain.

Margery Massena-Roach

I'm a mess
I am helpless
I'm drowning, the future looks so hazy
Please don't let me lose my mind, it feels like I might go crazy,
So I called on you to save me
And you gave me
Wings like an eagle
While changing my direction so I look to you for strength instead of
Looking to people
You pulled me off of the brink of evil
I felt so alone in this fight
But you were right
In the middle with me
I'm saved by grace, and there's no trace of where the adversary tried to
Sift me
This agony came in and stripped me
You helped me to let this thing go
For too long it had control
I was a pawn on someone's board, and I can't afford to lose my soul
In these broken pieces, only you could make me whole
Through Christ my will was broken and my battle was won
As I look to the hills from whence my help cometh from
Weeping endured for a night, morning is here, now joy has come
Though scarred by wounds so deep, it worked together for the best
And now I've been completely healed from my brokenness
Yes,
I have made it through the fire
Through the thicket and through the mire
I am a survivor!

For the Lord taketh pleasure in his people: he will beautify the meek with salvation.

(Psalm 149:4, KJV)

Reflecting His Beauty

Lord, draw me nearer to thee
So that I may reflect your beauty
It's not the apparel I wear
Or the length of my hair
But it's the salvation of Christ that defines my appearance as fair
Reveal yourself through me
So others may see
A spiritual beauty
And they'll know indeed
I'm worth far more than rubies
Let me sprout leaves
Like the fig tree
When summer is near
As I grow in the spirit and walk in Godly fear
Favor is deceitful, and beauty is vain:
But a woman that fears the Lord, she shall be praised
I want a gentle and quiet spirit
Not only to hear truth, but to live it
Beauty will change and fade like the lily
How far can I go if only outside is pretty?
You look at my heart; man looks at my skin

Margery Massena-Roach

You beautified me when you washed all my sins
Let the meekness in me pour out from within,
And may the lost catch a glimpse of your glory's brim
Men define beauty by what they see with their eyes,
But my beauty is Christ-likeness that comes from inside
When the world looks at me let them only see you
Pure and holy, tried and true
Cleanse my soul and make me new
Rest on my heart like morning dew
Give me holy boldness and fill me up with virtue
Let my feet be shod with the gospel of peace
My countenance changed when you set me free
No need for foundation or false eye lashes
I have joy for my mourning and beauty for ashes
Crown of glory and diadem
You were adored by three wise men
Born of a virgin in in Bethlehem
You showed me beauty that comes from within
It is a true beauty that goes deeper than skin.

Ye are the salt of the earth: but if the salt have lost his savor, wherewith shall it be salted? It is thenceforth good for nothing, but to be cast out, and to be trodden under foot of men. Ye are the light of the world. A city that is set on an hill cannot be hid. Neither do men light a candle, and put it under a bushel, but on a candlestick; and it giveth light unto all that are in the house. Let your light so shine before men, that they may see your good works, and glorify your Father which is in heaven.
(Matthew 5:13-16, KJV)

If Tombstones Could Talk

If I could see into my future, I wonder what I'd find.
Would I've been an achiever, would I've wasted time?
Would I've done much for Christ or sat there on a pew?
Would the souls that I'd won be of great or a few?
Would I have heard so much preaching and still be the same?
Would my life be different, would my mind have changed?
Would I've learned from my past or dwelled on mistakes?
Would I be a better person than I am today?
If I died in the future, what would be said?
Would they say I was Christ-like in the life that I led?
Would I have lived my life for more than myself?
Would I give without ceasing, was I selfless?
Would I be closer to Christ than I am today?
Would I stand on His promise, would His Word lead my way?
Would troubles make me bitter or would I be stronger?

Margery Massena-Roach

Would my passion increase, would I press in prayer longer?
Even though tombstones have limited space,
Here's what I'd hope my tombstone would say:
"Here lies a servant, a follower of Jesus Christ
She wanted to please God; He was first in her life
She lived life to the fullest with one precious goal,
To teach the true gospel and reach many souls
She had Christ-like compassion; she lived a life of holiness
She never stopped giving, she walked in her purpose."

Ye cannot drink the cup of the lord, and the cup of devils: ye cannot be partakers of the Lord's table, and of the table of devils.
(1 Corinthians 10:21, KJV)

All or Nothing (Spoken Word)

Give Him all or give Him nothing
Because it's not enough for you to just give Him some things
Come. Bring yourself as an offering
Give Him a broken heart and a contrite spirit
Not only worship from your lips but a life that lives it
And a heart that is in it
Monday through Sunday
On a quest for God, not just on one day
Some say
"I go to church" or "I'm a good person"
"I believe in God," or "I'm only human"
But God said, "I wish that you were hot or cold"
Because hanging in the middle has gotten too old
And to the lukewarm God said He will spew out their souls
So let go of the worldly things
And keep your eyes fixed on Him
Lay aside every weight and the sin
That does so easily beset you
Let Him make you a new
Creature and old things should pass
For the pleasures of this world are temporary, they fade and never last

Margery Massena-Roach

He said love not the world or things in it, so we shouldn't be attached
Know that a double minded man is unstable in all of his ways
We may be playing with the devil but the devil doesn't play
And though time may seem irrelevant, you might only have today.

This flesh is far from perfection
So this flesh must be placed under subjection
And we must pray and fast so we could maintain a connection
To Him
Every time we sin
It's like we bring Him
Back to Calvary
To adorn
Him with a crown of thorns
And nail Him back to a tree
For He
Was wounded for our transgressions, He was bruised for our iniquity
Jesus, please help us to die to the flesh daily!
And take the scales off of our eyes so we can see
How some of us have fallen asleep
And how we've
Reached the point where we can't even feel convicted
Because Satan has moved in and the Holy Spirit has been evicted
Some of us have become addicted
To sin, and live lives that are so conflicted
Choose this day whom you will serve,
Whether you will walk on the straight path or bend with the curve
It's either we flirt with the devil or give God the worship He deserves
Because no man can serve two masters
So which god have you been seeking after?

"He that is not with me is against me,"
Jesus said this in Matthew twelve verse thirty
The outside of the cup looks clean but first it's the inside that should
Not be dirty
The world feeds its lust and promotes seduction
Because it hates God and sound instruction
The Word says there's a way that seems right to a man but the end
Thereof is destruction.

The wolf is wearing sheep's clothes because he is a deceiver
He added one word to God's rule and converted Eve to a believer
Sin's penalty is death, so Jesus came as the Redeemer
The King became a servant, fully divine and fully man
He who shaped us,
Made us from dust,
Yet we pierced the potter's hands
The people wanted a king who came in riches, their blinded eyes
Couldn't understand
This picture
Was so much bigger
Than what they could see
His mission was to die for humanity
They said, "Is not this Jesus, the son of Joseph?" but He
Was like the ram
Caught in the thicket, Christ, the I Am That I Am
The Ultimate Lamb
And High Priest
The Lion of Judah, a gate for the sheep
The Bishop of Souls and the Horn of Salvation
The only solid foundation and Ruler of Creation

Margery Massena-Roach

The Chief Cornerstone, the desire of all nations
The offspring of David and sin's propitiation
He became the ransom for many, they called Him Messiah
He is the Last Adam, He is a soul purifier
And the Way, the Light, the Great Physician, and Rabbi
The Prince of Peace, Son of Man, Son of the Most High
King of kings, *Sh'ma Yis'ra'eil Adonai*
Eloheinu Adonai echad,
Yeshua Ha'Mashiach, we must choose God
He is true and He is holy but Satan is a fraud.

Jesus said, "Behold I stand at the door and knock"
All other ground is sinking sand; we must stand on Christ, the solid Rock
When our Lord cracks the sky, many heathens will bow in shock
Realizing that He has come just as so many have said
His eyes are as a flame of fire, He will have many crowns upon His Head
The very hand that pierced His side then will see that our Savior isn't Dead
He said they that worship Him must worship in spirit *and* in truth
Because even the devils believe in God and they also tremble too
God has called many women and men, yet His laborers are few
But we are the light of the world; a city set on a hill cannot be hid
Declare God's Word, sweeter than honey, the enemy's words are like Acid
Share that God gives oil of joy for mourning, that He gives beauty for Ashes
Our lives must be a testament to the masses
God called us to be above average

Breathe Life Speak Life

He said we are the salt of the earth
And if salt loses its savor then salt loses its worth
We must not just go to the house of worship; we must be the church
Jesus said if I be lifted up, I will draw all men unto me
And once He touches a life, there's no denying that He's mighty
Every ear needs to hear, this gospel is free
God's will is that all should repent
When you fall
Or you sit on the fence
The coach calls
It's time for you to get up; you've been sitting too long on the bench
His grace and mercy He extends
Jesus has called His people friends
Break down your walls
Surrender your all
And let the church say amen.

For the time will come when they will not endure sound doctrine; but after their own lusts shall they heap to themselves teachers, having itching ears; And they shall turn away their ears from the truth, and shall be turned unto fables. But watch thou in all things, endure afflictions, do the work of an evangelist, make full proof of thy ministry.

(2 Timothy 4:3-5, KJV)

The World's Jesus (Spoken Word)

I remember a time
When a husband and wife
Had two different beds on TV
But my, how things have changed so drastically
To the point where we need a sensory
Discretion sign as an advisory
On every television set.

You can't even get
Through a commercial without the hint of sex
As women willingly undress
For the love of money, I wonder, *what ever happened to self-respect?*
It seems that people will justify any deed for the purpose of a check
Nakedness is now called empowerment, tasteful art, and progress.

No one wants to be modest anymore

Breathe Life Speak Life

Conservative ways are too traditional and Bibles have become home
Decor
They say do what feels right, so we feed our lust like a kid in a candy
Store
Besides, it's the in-thing to be liberal
So the world has created its own truth and rejects the truth that is
Actually biblical
And God forbid, if you don't party or drink, people might not say it but
Think that your life must be really miserable!

The world's message is called "No Hate" and "Tolerance",
But they will hate you and debate with you and everyone would be
Hollering
If you stood for beliefs that Christians in the world used to believe in
And even
If you respectfully stand for the biblical truth
They will come at you
Like fire-breathing
Dragons, perspiring, and seething,
And put you on the front page of the papers for simply disagreeing
They will book you in jail with killers as if you have also stopped a
Heart from beating!

Believe in
The Word of God and they will say
It's not ok, that way is discriminatory
But it's funny that they're the first to take out baby Jesus on Christmas
Day to give him glory
It makes me think, *are we all reading the same Bible story?*

Because people are using the scriptures that they like to support their
Scripts
And then they pretend like the other scriptures that they dislike don't
Exist
Do you see how this conflicts?

It's a sign of the times
Every Bible-believing Christian is walking a thin line
As long as you hide the beliefs most disagree with then everything
Should be fine
Because if you dare to share the whole gospel, they will say you have a
Closed mind
And that you need to be educated, you're like those racists of old times
Our United States dollars still say, "In God We Trust"
But we have taken God out of the equation, and now it's really all
About us
And we glamorize rebels while critiquing Christians with disgust.

This world's Jesus has been enlightened, you see, he has no rules
He submits to our own sense of morality, the world's Jesus is cool
And he is so politically correct that he's a politically correct fool
The old Jesus is just too old-school
The world's Jesus would never offend!
And the world's Jesus doesn't stand out from the crowd, he blends.

Can I get an amen?
He is more like an appeasing friend
Than a savior
And don't worry, sinful behavior
Doesn't bother him, he will tell everyone to do exactly

What it is that makes them happy
He will then gladly
Bend his own rules to suit everyone, and lastly
The world's Jesus is more into giving gifts.

It's a shame that the world has dismissed
The true and living Jesus, Christ of the scriptures for this
Jesus that does not exist!
He's a false persona who will lead you to a pit
And feed you sweet lies while he facetiously pleads the Fifth
The world's Jesus is a myth because if the world's Jesus truly loved you
He would give you truth for your own benefit
Even if you don't like it, and he wouldn't put it through a filter.

It's like a mother who gives her kid bitter medicine when he is sick
She might say, "I know this doesn't taste good, but Baby, you need it"
And as her child you would receive it
Because you know that your mom would never harm you
And if she sees that you are in danger, she wouldn't stay quiet, she
Would alarm you
She wouldn't cheer you on if you are headed in the wrong direction
Because your mother really loves you, she would always provide
Correction
So how much more would the real Jesus do?
Like a good father should, He actually loves you
And He wouldn't tell you a lie, He gives...He is truth.

About the Author

Margery Massena-Roach aka Breathe Life Speak Life is a graduate of Hunter College. As a teenager, she was an Op-Ed Columnist for *The Sheepshead Bay Times* in which a poem she wrote was first featured. In college, Margery joined the Christian Club where she was highlighted in *The Hunter Envoy* for teaching engaging small group Bible studies. She was formerly the first female youth pastor of New Life Tabernacle Church, UPC in Brooklyn, NY, a congregation of 1500. She currently works in the field of Early Childhood Education and still serves in ministry. She has shared her poetry and the gospel at various events and continues to do so often. For inquiries, please send an email to **Paintwithwords20@gmail.com**. To connect with Margery and get updates on her work, find her on Facebook as **Breathe Life Speak Life.**

Made in the USA
Lexington, KY
23 December 2017